# SHADOW ACT

# SHADOW ACT

*An Elegy for Journalist
James Foley*

DANIEL BROCK JOHNSON

MCSWEENEY'S
POETRY SERIES

# McSWEENEY'S

SAN FRANCISCO

Printed in the United States.

ISBN: 978-1-95211-968-2

Cover design by Justin Carder

Cover photo by the author

2   4   6   8   10   9   7   5   3   1

www.mcsweeneys.net

*

*In memory of
James Wright Foley*

(1973–2014)

*

Tell me about a complicated man.
Muse, tell me how he wandered & was lost...

—*The Odyssey*,
translated by Emily Wilson

# CONTENTS

\*

*With all respects to heaven,*

\*

# Missing

There, then not: a late summer whiff
of something gone. It depended on the wind.
I checked the trash, after Ebele asked—
no maggots, no rancid fat globbing
the bin's lid—hunted through bushes, bellied
under the latticed front porch. Tuesday,
Wednesday: 85, 90 degrees. The stink, massive.
A squirrel, a raccoon? Too rank to be
a chickadee wind-swept from its nest.
My panic grew. Now, I think I know why.
I waded into shoulder-high hydrangeas,
greened with blooms, parted the branches—a blue
plastic bag, beer bottle cap, a skull-shaped
rock. Then I saw it—a patch of white,
matted there, sticks piercing the spongy form.
I covered my mouth & nose, retreated
to the bulkhead for leather gloves, a bandana,
& a small coal shovel. As I worked, I made out
hind legs, splayed, the orange & white
marbled fur—carrion beetles writhed, quaking,
once more, the belly of my neighbor's cat.
*What do I do with the body?* I asked Ebele.
This was the cat that leapt from a tree
onto the roof of the red Colonial on Delano
& survived for weeks, eluding firemen
who telescoped their ladder out, this the cat,

while I sat at my desk each morning to write,
that padded down the front steps
of my elderly neighbor's house, jumped the chainlink
& crossed the boulevard, stepping
between magnolias. *Your calico cat, I fear,*
*has died in my hydrangea bush*, I started the letter
to my bed-ridden neighbor. Though we needed
to get rid of the body, though the heat thickened
& soured, I spent hours laying down
my words, striking, double-striking them,
starting, again. This, I needed to get right.

*

*Wayfarer*


The night we slept with our windows open,
we woke to yellow leaves littering the bedroom floor,
filling our wine cups, puddling in our shoes.
Our room shone the color of an autumn swamp,
a slash of red where a boat moved off.


\*


We waited for her.

She crossed an expanse.
We charted her course.

She came by boat on a Tuesday.
Rather, she came by knife

& traveled light.
We waited for her

& she waited for us.
We called her Chance.

We call her Olanna.
She came on a Tuesday,

bright knife.

# Winter Daughter

Flags slap in slanting rain
& the trees on Poplar Street

tremble like cranial nerves.
To keep the heat,

I seal off our bedroom windows
with plastic sheeting,

even then we bicker
over one or two degrees.

A cry strikes flint in the half-light.
Ebele clutches our newborn,

curses the draft. We have known
& been cold before, I think.

Better yet, I will teach
our winter daughter—

I mean, I will teach
our *daughter winter*—

to swig Scotch from a flask,
to pull through ice a thrashing pike.

# Photograph: Roslindale, 2010

Standing in our kitchen, Jim clutches Olanna, at 6 months,
to his chest like a bundle of forwarded mail. The top of
Olanna's pink-knit hat crests above his shoulder. Jim cracks a
toothy gambler's grin—it's his mother's smile & *her* mother's
smile before that. These things, they're neither created nor
destroyed.[1]

---

1   First, he left his mother's womb, black as the sea floor at 2,500
feet. Next, Chicago, City of Big Shoulders, Hog Butcher for the World:
James left in a green Pontiac station wagon, suckling at his mother's
breast.

## Glinrose
### —Ragged Islands, Nova Scotia


Morning fog.
We pick thistle for the table.

This & if—
I set them down

to walk the rocky coast
strewn with buoys

& traps, lugging
twenty-seven stones

on my back.
Frigates wing past.

Light & waves cut us off
from where we came.

Here where entire ships
of men disappear—

this bright weight,
my sleeping daughter.

When the path returns,
we mean to return.

Half moon. Rising sable tide.

# Daybook: July 19

This journal—started on the 517th day of Jim's capture on a summer morning when my office smells faintly of skunk—is a study of absence, presence, & the shining, alchemical ever-presence of absence.[2]

---

2   He left his room at home a museum of comic books, swimming medals, rock posters, cached away nudie mags, baseball cards, & Granite State Quiz Bowl Challenge ribbons.

## Daybook: August 17

I'm reading *Thank You for Your Service*, a book on the trauma of war & the scars it leaves. After a roadside bomb blasts off in Baghdad, one soldier describes his buddy bursting into "pink mist."[3]

---

3    With a stuffed Army duffel & stickered trunk, Jim left for Milwaukee, aka Brew City, home of Marquette University. He left the Law Library for the rugby field, the rugby scrum for the Avalanche Bar. His arm in a cast, he left the 'Lanche at 3 AM, bloodied, being dragged, after brawling with friends & getting trapped under a beer-stained pool table, where he took kick after kick in the ribs & chin, until Marco freed him & pulled him, laughing, out onto Wells Street.

*catalogue of accidents*


the day
Luka learned to walk
proud
holding an apple
he crashed down
wood stairs
hard
barrel-rolling
half a flight
Luka cried & cried
wild sucking air
between sobs
clung to his mother
choked down milk
as if we'd
thrown him
ourselves


\*


praise blind
fucking luck
praise his skull intact
his neck his back
praise ignorance
praise belief

praise the part-time gods
of Poplar Street

pardoned
we cry
& kiss our boy
loose wild
promises into the sky
pour Prosecco
let the specter
of ruin
skitter away
we laugh & laugh
the moon is up

# Tuesday on Poplar Street

*Don't—*
cries Luka
as her car pulls out.
*Love you!*
Olanna shouts
& skips
inside. The kids
& I lay out
train tracks,
bridge pillars,
the sprawling
wheelhouse
& pry the top
off a stalled
red engine to slip
fresh batteries
inside.

Sliced apples.
Lemonade.
This is our book
of days.

*

Passing the door,
I spy Ebele's
Honda parked,
again, at the curb,
as if the hour
has been rewound,
the late August sky
re-divined.

Barefoot,
I step onto
the porch, smile
& wave. Her
door falls
open. Shoulders
slack, eyes cast
down, she rises
in heels from
her car but
won't approach.

*What's wrong?*
I ask & touch
my wife's face.
Low sobs
lift her white
ruffled blouse.
The kids
press against
the storm door,

a train in each
of Luka's hands.

*It's Jimmy*, you
say. *It's Jim.*

*

# glimmerings

"It's the little things that keep us going but how quickly we try to forget the fact they are holding us interminably as hostages using a process we have only the faintest glimmerings of."

—James Foley in his Libyan prison journal, April 2012

## 1.

*We went to Brega on April 5th to get close to the frontlines. We never imagined how our lives would change. Our foolishness gives me nightmares. We got in a red bus & drove ahead to the last checkpoint. Some teens told us Gaddafi troops were 300 meters away but we thought it was impossible.*

Now that Jim's gone-but-not-gone, here-but-not-here, I sit, from time to time, in front of these letters that he smuggled out of a Libyan prison in his shoe. I let my eyes roam the teeming sea of words, the script dizzyingly small.

*We watched the scout bus & some pickups drive 200 meters more & turn when two Gaddafi trucks came firing. We pressed ourselves close to the ground as bullets zipped overhead. I heard Anton yell "help help," but I couldn't even raise my head. I yelled "Are you okay?" He said "No," more bullets, I called again. Nothing*

## 2.

Page 1 of Jim's letter is double-columned, crammed with blue text. You can see that he's conserving space, printing neatly on unlined paper. This alone is remarkable, surely a sign of duress.

Graphology, a science founded in the sixteenth century, is the study of handwriting to determine a person's psychological state at the time of writing. Graphologists assess qualities like movement, spacing, & form. Its seminal text, published in Italian in 1622, is titled *How to Know, Through a Handwritten Letter, the Personality & Nature of the Author.*

While he was a middle school teacher at Lowell Elementary, Jim was a poster boy for poor penmanship, so much so that the headmaster gave Jim a Tinsley's Penmanship workbook, the student edition, to improve his handwriting.

# 3.

If you look closely, numbers 1, 2, 3, & 4, pepper the body of the text, suggesting that Jim penned page 1 of this letter over four sessions, during his 44-day captivity. The first page, you can see, has been creased down the middle between the two columns & three times vertically, so that Jim could fold & hide the letter in his shoe.

After teaching middle school in Phoenix as a recent college graduate, Jim plumbed his experiences to write a prize-winning short story. The protagonist, Mr. Foley, receives an anonymous letter. From her distinct handwriting & punctuation, Foley recognizes it as coming from Joanna, founder of the "We Hate Mr. Foley Club":

> *Mr. Foley You are not the boss of this school so don't try to boss us. Give back our pencils now. And please go back where you came from, (note the use of comma) or else From some body*

## 4.

The sign-off of Joanna's letter evokes Emily Dickinson's "I'm Nobody! Who are you?" In her lifetime, the reclusive poet wrote more than 1,800 poems, many on the flaps, backs, & scraps of envelopes she received in the mail, including this one—

*A not admitting / of the Wound / Until it grew so /
wide / That all my / Life had Entered it –...*

One contemporary likened her handwriting to "fossil bird-tracks."

During his Libyan captivity, Jim scrawled micro-notes on a series of flattened cigarette boxes, lined hash marks on the cinder block walls of his cell to track the passing days.

\*

## Photograph: El Desemboque, Mexico, 1999

On top of a coastal dune, Jim sits cross-legged with a notebook in his lap. Brewers cap flipped backward, he's wearing silk basketball shorts. I can never remember him so still. Doesn't a body in motion *stay* in motion? The Gulf sun spills his shadow like Oaxacan ink.[4]

---

4    Jim left his classroom at Lowell Elementary, sweating through his chalk-dusted polo in the Phoenix heat, swearing to himself to never return. He left when the bell rang. He left after being beaten & bested. He left after whipping chalk at Antonio during a long division lesson, after quaking at his desk, after sucking down a bummed smoke with animal panic outside the teacher's lounge. He left only to return, again & again.

# Homecoming

When Maureen stepped out, Jim sacked her closet
for a candy-striped tube top, A-line skirt,
size-10 nude pumps, plum lip gloss,
bangles, & a boar bristle brush to push
through his gelled-back, chestnut hair.
He let loose a slimming breath & wriggled,
inch by inch, into the Spandex top,
broad shoulders busting stitches, dusted
his cheeks with champagne blush,
& rounded up his tawdry gaggle
of first-time drag queens, wobbly in heels.
*¡Vamanos, chicas!* he commanded
while passing a flask of tequila,
before speeding off to Sky Harbor Airport.
Rick, matronly, reeking of Chanel,
sparked up a Camel Light.
Don, svelte, head shaved, penciled in
a smoky, wavering brow.
The bright August heat kissed away
Jim's foundation. Drivers gawked.
A trucker on the Hohokam honked
& blew a lilting kiss.

When I stepped off my Pittsburgh flight,
chatting up Ashley, an ASU student,
high-pitched cries of *DJ! O-o-o-o-o' DJ!*

sang out from the waiting area
like a welcoming committee
of eunuchs & hornbill cranes.
I wheeled around, only to be swallowed
by a swarm of kisses, pinches,
linebacker hugs, falsetto cries,
& beefy fingers mussing
my bottle-blond hair. That was the summer
of my solo trip to Spain, summer
of my mother's diagnosis,
summer of waking to find Mom gone
in her bathrobe, only to be returned
by local police. I wanted to be flayed,
wanted to be saved.

We headed off to baggage claim,
where Don lay, spread-eagle,
in a white jersey dress, circling
the baggage carousel, where Rick
in a black evening gown & beaded beret
plucked my bags from the carousel,
& Jim, Jim pulled up curbside,
windows cranked down, his VW Fox
booming Tribe Called Quest.

In the Summer of 1998,
this is what it meant to be blessed—
to be spirited away by B-grade drag queens
down Camelback & Indian School,
to pass a joint, its tip gone pink with lipstick,

& evanesce in a mist of jasmine,
iris, amber, & sandalwood.

# Photograph: Phoenix, 1998

A class picture from Lowell Elementary. Jim (fourth row, far left) listed as "Mr. Foley" stands ramrod straight in a white Oxford next to the Arizona state flag. Mario (row 2) crosses his eyes. Reuben (row 3) inflates his cheeks like a puffer fish. Jim tenses his jaw, as a strobe lights the scene, again & again.[5]

---

5   After getting reamed for his own sophomoric efforts, Jim left John Edgar Wideman's fiction workshop crestfallen & reported to the Amherst Pub. Two Jamesons in hand, Shauna threw her arm around him, told him to shake off the drubbing & dubbed their fellow MFA candidates "My Fragile Associates."

# Protect Me from What I Want
### –Havana, Cuba


could have been the motto
inked above his wrist—
a prayer, a plea,

a sans serif reminder to self.
The body is a temple
awash in island light.

Protect me from lust.
The body a Cuban dance hall.
Rum on the tongue. Tom-

toms. Marimbas. Pressing Lourdes
close in a short, lace dress.
¡Ay, Havana! Protect me

if you want. Our guidebook
declared the shimmering bay
slapping against the Malecón

too tainted for swimming.
With a Cristal bottle raised,
Jim stroked on his back

through breaking waves.

# Photograph: Havana, Cuba, 1999

In a poppy-red t-shirt, Jim powers a borrowed rickshaw over
potholed streets, past women in neon Lycra strolling the
Malecón, past a guitarist singing, *Hay locuras que son poesía. Hay
locuras sin nombre.*[6]

---

6   Buzzing on caffeine & nicotine, Jim left a night class on conflict
reporting, carrying a notebook full of tips on freelancing—"Avoid being
photographed with combatants"; "When being fired at, run in a zigzag
fashion"—& a list of equipment to take into the field:

| | |
|---|---|
| Canon EOS-7500 D (two bodies) | 28 - 200 lens |
| shotgun mic | extra batteries & chargers |
| a dozen memory cards | anti-ballistic flak jacket |
| XL Kevlar helmet | laptop |
| cell phone & audio recorder | waterproof gear bags |
| 2 external hard drives | satellite phone |
| Arabic dictionary | tripod |
| passport & copies | St. Francis De Sales prayer card |

# Foley Artist: Sound Effects for an Unmade Short Film

FX 1:   A classroom door, like a pistol shot, bangs open then shut

2:      High desert wind

3:      Shouts, scuffling of feet

4:      A 35-mm camera shutter clicks

5:      *Who's gonna clean all this shit up?*

6:      Clattering of laptop keys

7:      Repeated striking of a lighter's flint

8:      Traffic on W. 18th Street

9:      A paper bag rumples, wind off the lake

10:     Squealing tires, buckling of metal & plastic

11:     *Now boarding Lufthansa Flight 423 to Istanbul*

12:     A noise like Black Cat firecrackers popping off over a low stone wall

13:     Throaty bass from car speakers

14:     The doorbell buzzes[7]

---

7     Jim swung through the door of his Pilsen apartment, midday, to pick up groceries—eggs, milk, white rice, jalapeños, sandwich bread, cold cuts, ginger ale. Minutes later, he crashed his Civic, while reading Chomsky in Chicago traffic.

## Nothing Is More Beautiful than
## the Ruin of a Beautiful Thing

He's looking down at the keys in his hand

    he'd offer later

It doesn't matter.
The light is liquid as it is

Call it thieves' light.
    All shadows are final

like dimes in water.

on

        our knees

      we'll order sweet plantains

& pepper steak,
        I'll curse

the Year of the Ox.


He'll raise his can of Tsingtao

                                                                                           

&                                         *die before us!*

# Knight of Swords
### –Ukrainian Village, Chicago, 2001

I hired a Polish soothsayer
who advertised her services
in teal neon on Ashland Avenue–

*Tarot. Numerology Charts.*
*Aura Cleansing in 21 Days*
*or Your Money Back!*

Aleksandra the Seer
popped open her card table
& lay a velvet cloth on top.

Hand in hand, she sat
with bookish partygoers
hopped up on pot brownies

& gin. She warned José
of a seven-year hex. Linna,
she divined, would never find love

in Illinois. Sage smoke
swirled. Candles flickered.
Aleksandra fingered a deep

crescent riving Jim's palm.

*

You're crossing a trash-strewn riverbed. I see a car in flames. You're running towards it. God is an animal inside you, am I right? You'll lose yourself under a red sky. I see you praying on your knees. You've taken a different name. Your time is nearly up. Would you like me to go on?

## Photograph: New York City, 2001

Snow blown into heaps. Spires from St. John the Divine stretch
out of frame. It's an hour past dawn on the Upper West Side.
Jim's plastic New Year's hat shines like a crumpled Sapporo can.
Two pretty cousins squeeze between us, both with long braids
& black coats. How do you pass the days in the absence of
light? Sing the names of the women you've known.[8]

---

8    Security deposits & unpaid bills, Jim left behind, & copies of his
novel-in-progress titled *The Cowhead Revelations* & then, *Notes to a Fellow
Educator* &, later, *A Letter to James Foley About the Type of Students You Will
Be Receiving as I Am Leaving the Classroom to Re-Dedicate Myself to Educa-
tion.* He left Rachel. He left Yago's sister. He left Charlene & then he left
his novel in a drawer.

*

# glimmerings

## 5.

Jim ends page 1 of his Libya letter with a litany of mixed thanks: *To call one's mother after disappearing for 17 days, to see one's passport, a judge who gives you two more weeks without telling you. [...] To receive fresh packs of cigarettes, boxes of juice, to wash one's jeans after 20 days, one's shirt still spotted with blood after three sinks. To learn the Fatiha & hope inner peace will carry me outside the bars. To be released for one hour into the sunshine & see the faces, eyes closed to the sun.*[9]

---

9    Packing for a red-eye, Jim left this phone message: "Hey Johnson. Hey brother. I'm...umm...taking off to Libya tomorrow. I'm covering a couple stories on the anniversary, then I'll be back in May. I hope all's well. I know it is. Happy Valentine's Day. Give Olanna a little hug for me. Umm, &, I hope—well, I'll try to catch you on Skype when I'm over there, bro."

# 6.

In 1862, Walt Whitman was reading *The New York Tribune* when he came across the name "First Lieutenant G.W. Whitmore [sic], Company D," listed among the Union wounded & dead. In a panic, he packed a bag & fled Brooklyn for Washington, D.C., to find his brother George.

Whitman ghosted through camp after camp, filling one note-book, then another—Washington, D.C., to Aquia Landing to Falmouth, Virginia—encountering Union soldiers, living & dead, like Thomas Haley, laid out in a cot. Whitman writes:

*June 18*

> *In one of the Hospitals I find Thomas Haley, Co., M, Fourth New York Cavalry—a regular Irish boy, a fine specimen of youthful physical manliness—shot through the lungs—inevitably dying—came over to this country from Ireland to enlist—has not a single friend or acquaintance here—is sleeping soundly at this moment, (but it is the sleep of death)—has a bullet-hole straight through the lung...*[10]

---

10  Rumbling through a high mountain pass with Alpha Company 2–327th Infantry 1st 101st Brigade, Jim's convoy came under fire. Doors flung open, camera rolling, Jim sprinted, low, toward the Humvee ahead of them, now flaming, a limp American soldier lying roadside, as fellow troops shouted into field radios, before their caravan sped away, still taking fire, gravel flying.

## 7.

In *The Return*, Hisham Matar's memoir about his father's decades-long disappearance at the hands of the Gaddafi regime, a political prisoner in Abu Salim counts the bloodied watches & wedding bands as he removes them from massacred prisoners. He does this so he can bear witness, if he himself survives. He tallies 1,270 dead.

Another prisoner, an uncle of Matar's, steals a pillowcase, plucks out the threads, & laces the fabric with his own poems. He then rolls the cloth & sews it into his waistband, a prayer belt of words. What's handmade becomes sacred, I've learned, after its maker is gone.

*

*Four Foreign Journalists Held in Libya*
*–April 7, 2011*


Forces loyal to Col. Muammar el-Gaddafi have detained journalists in Libya, the *GlobalPost* news organization said Thursday, among them one of its contributing reporters, James Foley.

... They were taken on Tuesday while reporting on the outskirts of Brega, an oil town in eastern Libya. Their whereabouts on Thursday were unknown.

... *GlobalPost*, an online news publication, said that the other journalists were Clare Morgana-Gillis, an American freelancer who has reported for *The Atlantic*, & two photographers, Manu Brabo of Spain & Anton Hammerl of South Africa.

–Elizabeth A. Harris
for *The New York Times*

*War Reporter Kidnapped a Second Time*
*—January 3, 2012*

The family of James Foley, a Boston-based foreign correspon-
dent who was abducted in Libya in 2011, said Wednesday that
he was kidnapped again on Thanksgiving Day, this time while
reporting from Syria, & remains missing.

*—The Boston Globe*

# Celebration

"Four Foreign Reporters, Including *GlobalPost's* Foley, Freed in
Libya"
          —*PBS NewsHour*, May 18, 2011

The governor dubbed it James Foley Day.
We toasted Jim in a white party tent.
Hoisting a beer bottle, he said,

*I went to see the elephant.*
I drank gin & tonics on that perfect lawn.
Jim held Olanna in his arms.

*Come with me, Sweetie,* he whispered
into her curls, *I'll take you,*
*if you want, to go see the elephant.*

We toasted Jim in a white party tent.
He stared off & through us
like he saw something we couldn't—

a flashing mirror, a wisp of smoke—
whatever it was, he didn't say.
Jim's mom handed him gifts

for each of the guests.
I couldn't open mine for a year.
We toasted Jim in a white party tent.

The governor dubbed it James Foley Day.
*I'd love to stay*, he explained,
*but I've got to get back to see the elephant.*

# Sparrows

*—composed during James Foley's 636-day captivity in Syria,*
*including lines from his Libyan prison journal*


Rockets concuss. Guns rattle off.
Dogs in a public square
feed on dead horses.

I don't know, Jim, where you are.
When did you last see
birds? The winter sky in Boston

is gray with flu. Newspapers,
senators, friends, even your mom
on *Good Morning America*—

no one knows where you are.
It's night, cold & bruised,
where you are. Plastic binds

your hands. You wait & pray, pray & wait,
but this is where the picture goes gray.
We don't know, Jim, where you are.

\*

In the absence of sparrows: a crowd of friends & family gather
in Rochester, New Hampshire, to recite the holy rosary.

*

*We met an American through the electrical socket.*
*He told us the story of a dog*
*painted red, green, & black & let loose*
*at the police station. I imagine*
*the dog is still running...*

*

*Clare & I sat 12 days in a cell praying—night.*
*To help us—today. To help us. Mr. Shabbani.*
*—the plane—the Libyan clock... two boys*
*down toward the fighting—my mom [...],*
*maybe my father. To help us. To help us.*

*

We keep your picture on the kitchen table, pack of
    American Spirits,
airplane bottle of Scotch, a copy of *Krapp's Last Tape.*

Don't get me wrong; we expect you back. Skinny, feral,
coffee eyes sunken but alive, you've always come back,
    from Iraq,

Syria, Afghanistan, even Libya after Gaddafi's forces

captured & held you for 44 days. You tracked time scratching

marks with your zipper on prison walls, scrawling notes
    on cigarette
boxes, reciting *Al-Fatiha* with other prisoners. Then, you called.

*DJ, it's Jimmy...I'm in New Hampshire, brother!* I wanted
to break your fucking nose. We ate lobster rolls, instead,

on a picnic bench by Boston Harbor. You made a quick round
of TV shows, packed your camera & Arabic phrasebook.

You skipped town on a plane to Turkey. We talked once.
You said you'd play it safe. But the connection was lost.

            *


*Walking ahead on my own through the desert,*
*as if compelled by a magnet is insane.*
*But a day had to be measured—*
*in risk.*

            *


In the absence of sparrows: American journalist James Foley
    disappeared after being taken captive by armed gunmen
    near Aleppo, Syria on Thanksgiving Day.

            *

*We went to Brega on April 5th.*
*Our foolishness gives me*
*nightmares. We got in a red bus.*
*Some teens told us*
*our nightmares. Gaddafi*
*came firing. I yelled,* Sahafa!
*I couldn't raise my head.*
*Anton, Anton said, No.*

\*

In the absence of sparrows: our house burns blue with news.

\*

*Strange tantric music played in the truck.*
*The man took off my shoes as if to beat me.*
My grandfather fought the Italians
from a horse, *my interrogator said.*

\*

Winter solstice, 1991. You turned donuts,
drinking beers, in a snowy public lot next to the lake.
Girls yelped. You cranked the Pixies louder, cut the lights,
& steered Billy's grandma's Chrysler onto the
    Winnipesaukee ice.
The moon flamed bright as a county coroner's light.
You revved the station wagon's engine. Billy tied
a yellow ski rope off the hitch, flashed a thumbs up,

& you punched the gas—5, 15, 20, 25 miles per hour—
towing Billy, skating in high top sneakers,
across the frozen lake. Chill air filled his lungs.
Billy pumped his fist. You torqued the wheel left.
Triumphant, you honked & flashed the lights.
You took a swig of Heineken & wheeled
the wood-paneled station wagon in a wide-arcing turn
to pick up Billy, bloodied but standing. Your friends
named you the High King of Foolish Shit.
The nose of Billy's grandma's Chrysler broke the ice.
You jammed it into reverse. Bald tires spinning,
you flung yourself from the car. In seconds, it was gone.
You gave Billy's grandma a potted mum
& a silver balloon. Standing on her screened-in porch,
you mumbled an apology. *What am I supposed to do now?*
she asked. *What the hell do I do now?*

*

*Tripoli is a series of bars & cells,*
*separated by locks & keys.*
*Tripoli is a series of bars*
*& cells, separated by locks*
*& keys. I've become a series*
*of bars & cells, separated*
*by locks & keys.*

*

In the absence of sparrows: when falling snow, out the window,
    looks like radio waves, your face appears, your baritone

53

laugh.

*

Mock executions, electricity, whips, broken
fingers from Kalashnikovs. Mamoud said,
They caught a video of me feeding *The Green Book*
to my cow. I had no other form of protest.

*

*I was ashamed of myself.*
*I went far enough*
*to be in serious danger*
*but not to get much*
*footage beside running.*
*I'm doing a complete autopsy on my life.*

*

*August 31, 2004*

We read Abbie Hoffman, *1968*, watched Panther
    documentaries,
*The Weather Underground*, & packed our bandanas,
first aid kits, fat markers, maps, & signs for New York City.
A31, they called it, a day of direct action, a time to heave
    ourselves

on the gears of an odious machine. We marched, drumming

& chanting, half a million strong, through the streets
of Lower Manhattan. *Worst President Ever, A Texas Village Has
    Lost Its Idiot.*
Protestors carried a flotilla of flag-covered coffins.

We hoisted homemade signs & cried out, *Whose streets?
    Our streets?
No justice, no peace!* I'd packed sandwiches, water, mapped
    restrooms
along the parade route, inked the hotline for Legal Services
on your forearm & mine. You, my feral half-brother,

packed only a one hitter, notepad, & pen.
When the parade snaked past the New York Public Library,
we peeled off to confront a mass of cops in riot gear
blocking entry with batons drawn. We took position

on the library steps. Stone-still, inches from police, we held
    our signs
stamped with a student gagged by a padlock & chain.
I could feel breath on my neck. We narrowly escaped arrest,
then streamed toward The Garden, a ragtag troop of 200.

We evaded barricades. Cut down alleys. At Herald Square,
only blocks from the Republican Convention, cops on mopeds
cut us off. They rolled out a bright orange snow fence,
hundreds of yards long, then zip-cuffed us, one by one.

I called Ebele. You called your brother, set to be married
in just three days. His best man, you were headed to jail.

*I'll be there Friday for the golf outing,* you vowed, a cop cutting
your phone call short. They took you first. Threw you on a
   city bus

headed to Pier 14 on the Hudson, a giant garage stinking
of axle grease & gasoline. Stepping off the bus,
I scanned hundreds of faces staring through chainlink,
newly erected & topped with concertina wire.

I couldn't find you. I can't. They transferred me, in soapy light,
to the Tombs, Manhattan's city jail, & freed me after 24 hours.
I peered in Chinese restaurants, seedy Canal Street bars,
called your cell phone from a payphone, trekked to
   Yago's apartment

in Spanish Harlem, eager to crack beers, to begin weaving
the story we would always tell. You weren't there.
Waiting outside the Tombs, I missed my flight home.
Waiting, I smoked your cigarettes on the fire escape.

They held you & held you. You are missing still. I want to
   hold you.
Beauty is in the streets, my brother. Beauty is in the streets.


   *

*Prison is a world of small miracles.*
*To wash your jeans after 20 days.*
*To call one's mother after disappearing.*
*To eat couscous & watermelon.*

*To scrub blood still spotting your shirt*
*after three sinks.*

\*

*They took off my blindfold.*
*I'd kept my notes in my shoes–*
*Truly these are the last days.*
*Part of me wants to witness*
*what the end will be, to report it.*

\*

In the absence of sparrows: trash fires, a call to prayer. Dusk.
Rockets whistling, plastic bags taking flight.

In the absence of sparrows: all of a sudden, you appear.
Standing before a cinder block wall, you're holding a video
camera with a boom mic & wearing a bulletproof vest.

In the absence of sparrows: the front-page story says you've
been missing since November 22, 2012. Everything else it
doesn't say.

In the absence of sparrows: you simply wandered off, pockets
stuffed. The door to your apartment is open still—

*glimmerings*

8.

With a jeweler's loupe in hand, I bring my eyes even closer to
Jim's prison journal. *On the way my money was stolen* . . . His words
become letters. The letters dance into swirls & hooks—*Nicar made
a lamp out of a sardine can.* I see the woven cotton fibers of the page.
Its edges fringed with dirt.

Page 3 of Jim's Libya letter, the strangest & most beautiful of all,
burns a cool blue-white, the color of a midnight snowfield. In the
header, a crescent moon floats next to a small crest.

*3/5 They brought the best meal of captivity—couscous & watermelon.
They said the flag is flying in Tajora. Zawara is rumored to be free & the
revolutionaries controlling the Tunisian border. Truly these are the last
days. Rashid was freed more to follow. I feel at peace, if I am freed first
or with my Libyan brothers ...*

## 9.

To scratch an ashen line on the wall, to record events on paper—these acts alone, now tether Jim to me across space & time. What's the distance between us now from the moment Jim wrote these letters? 4,446 miles & 3,439 days—or 10 years, 6 months, & 29 days.

# 10.

"One of the first things that met my eyes in camp, was a heap of feet, arms, legs, &c. under a tree in front of a hospital," Whitman writes to describe the scene he encountered outside of Lacy House. On December 29th at the winter camp of the Army of the Potomac, Whitman makes a discovery.

It turns out that George—a carpenter-turned-Union foot soldier, who survived Antietam, Bull Run, Fredericksburg, & even being captured by the Confederate Army at the Battle of Poplar Springs Church—was recuperating from no more than a "slightly wounded cheek."

"When I found dear brother George, & found that he was alive & well, O you may imagine how trifling all my little cares & difficulties seemed."[11]

---

11 *This is James Foley reporting from Benghazi, Libya,* he states, staring into his own video camera, sunglasses pulled back on his head, trancey music blaring from a bullhorn held aloft in the background. *The mood in Benghazi swings between celebration & chaos today, a day after Western forces began air strikes on Gaddafi tanks south of the city limits. As the air strikes continued this morning on a column of armored vehicles 30 kilometers south, rebel soldiers packed into a square in the city center, spraying the air with victory shots.*

# 11.

In *The ISIS Hostage*, Daniel Rye Ottosen details his captivity in Syria alongside Jim & 17 others, as well as the fraternity that developed. Daniel, a Danish gymnast-turned-war-photographer, recounts being chained by the guards & hung from the ceiling for days, even trying to take his own life. "Fuck," he pleads & prays, "you can do whatever you like to me; hit the soles of my feet, whip my back, just don't hang me up without water again..."

Daniel recalls meeting Jim for the first time. He "noticed James's long toes & that he also had a scar around one of his ankles." He develops an immediate fondness for Jim & his innate clumsiness. Later, he watches an unmasked guard zip-tie Jim's tongue: "While he stood in front of James & put a plastic cable around his tongue, several of the hostages paid close attention to his (captor's) appearance."

When it becomes clear that Daniel is going to be freed, he & Jim hatch a plan. Jim drafts a letter on scraps of trash for Daniel to smuggle out. After they decide that it's too dangerous for Daniel to hide the letter in his underwear, he decides to memorize it.

When Daniel looks at the three-page note to Jim's family, he becomes dismayed—"James' i's looked like z's & his handwriting was almost illegible." Jim, instead, begins to dictate the letter, line by line to Daniel in a hushed voice in a corner of their cell, "Dear friends & family, I remember long walks with Mom, traveling to the mall with Dad..."

\*

*Islamist Militants Execute N.H. Reporter James Foley*
*–August 24, 2014*

James Foley, a freelance war correspondent from New Hampshire, was killed at the hands of the Islamic State militant group, which distributed a video that said the apparent beheading was retaliation for recent U.S. airstrikes in Iraq, U.S. officials said late Tuesday.

The officials told the Associated Press that they believe it is Foley in the video, bringing to a tragic end a saga that began when Foley was kidnapped in Syria in November 2012.

*We have never been prouder of our son Jim,* his mother, Diane, said in a message posted on a Facebook page his supporters had set up. *He gave his life trying to expose the world to the suffering of the Syrian people. We implore the kidnappers to spare the lives of the remaining hostages. Like Jim, they are innocents.*

–James Anderson & Bryan Bender
for *The Boston Globe*

[　　]¹²

---

12   To go missing. To be disappeared. To absent oneself in the truest sense, so you can't be found on a map. To friends & family, who prayed for him, who wrote him letters they would never send, Jim was alive & dead at the same time. Laughing & obliterated.

# August 19th

They say *New Hampshire man.*
They say *James Foley.*
They say *at the hands of the Islamic State.*
*Thanksgiving Day,* they say.
They say *Syria.*
They say *unmarked car* & *caliphate.*
*It is unclear,* they say.
*It is apparent.*
They say *freelance reporter.*
They say *James Foley.*
They say *black-clad captor* & *knife.*
*It is still possible,* they say.
*It is reported.*
They say *faded yellow.*
They say *ribbon* & *priest.*
They say *James Foley.*
They say, they say,
*we believe.*

# Daybook: August 31

Ebele dreamt of a giant tire raft carrying Jim & Philip Seymour Hoffman across a vast rippling plane of ocean. A paradise dream, it seems. That same night Olanna woke startled, scream- ing, *There's a horse in my room!*[13]

---

13 Anti-aircraft missiles exploding overhead that night, Jim tweeted, *Prayers over rocket fire Brega.* Then, he disappeared. On NPR, CBS, CNN, ABC, they reported him missing, *A New Hampshire journalist, James Foley, reportedly went missing outside of Brega, Libya today after being abducted in a truck.* Rifle-butted by a Gaddafi loyalist, he got hauled off with Clare & Manu, left Anton bleeding out in the sand.

# September 3rd

*I've been contacted by James Foley*
*& he wants to speak to you,*
the psychic typed, late at night,

just days after my face
appeared in *The Boston Globe.*
*John & Diane aren't open*

*to meeting with me*
*but his brother Michael is.*
So that's what psychics do

to drum up business,
they trawl the local papers
for stories of six-car pileups,

plane crashes, chemical
spills, kidnappings, beheadings,
& missing kin. Then,

they state the impossible.[14]

---

14  Every time he left, Jim left less & less behind. A joke. A book. *The Unabridged Journals of Sylvia Plath* with a hasty inscription scrawled on the title page.

# Inshallah

*–for Diane & John Foley*

When it was over,
though it would never be over,

Jim's mom sent a gift
to our house,

a chrome lamp & candles,
a tornado lantern

or hurricane lamp. It depends
what you call

that black wall of water,
skirling & rising,

that takes what it wants:
cars, refrigerators,

cows, wedding
photos, birth records—

*inshallah—*
your firstborn son.

When it was over,
though it would never be over,

as it would never be
*before* again, only *after*,

as the rains, the rains
would never be the same

rains or lashing waves—
I struck a match

against the flooding dusk,
then, again,

& hung the lamp.

## Daybook: December 26

ISIS, Okwui told me on Christmas day, while we sipped whiskey by the fire pit, *is trying to sell Jim's body for a million dollars.*

## Tenderness & Rage:
## A Suite in G Major

In the throes of loss,

*

I sidearm a wine glass against the wall,

*

spray of diamonds & Chardonnay.

*

A Brazilian orchid I grind to its roots

*

in the garbage disposal.

*

Words always fail me

*

and mostly I fail,

\*

mostly I fail them.

\*


But, then, there are mornings, mornings like this, when I ferry my three-year-old son to ballet in Boston's South End, past brownstones dusted white, Bach's Cello Suites breathing through the Honda's speakers. In my hand, I cup red raspberries in winter, supple, still wet from rinsing. I offer one, then two, hold out my hand to my son, who takes the tip of my finger into his mouth, lipping my offering. He eats the raspberries, humming, it's snowing, he eats them all.

*

*glimmerings*

12.

More than anything I want to touch & smell Jim's letter, but
I have only a digital copy of it. Five JPEGs, that's it. The inkjet
facsimile I spread on my oak desk smells new, nearly scentless.

To place my hand on the page where Jim placed his is what I want.
To suck into my lungs the ink, sweat, cigarette smoke, prison dust,
& pressed cotton fibers—to breathe Jim in, again.

## 13.

Emily Dickinson, a nineteenth-century New Englander, practiced thrift, took to heart the advice, "Preserve the backs of old letters to write upon." She scrawled her envelope poems around wax seals, over the names of telegraph companies, & further divided her scraps of paper into additional columns & rows. To "capture," meaning here, the art of gathering up all the fragments, so that not everything is lost.[15]

---

15  Jim left Libya for Turkey & Turkey for Syria, for Aleppo, Sirte & Saraqeb, where his videos came back chronicling whole cities leveled by gunfire & shell blasts, where he filmed Dar al Shifa Hospital getting bombed, where he stood bedside & interviewed a thirteen-year-old boy, who'd been hit by a bomb dropped from a helicopter as he stood in a breadline.

# 14.

On page 5, the last, Jim returns, again, to the wound of getting captured, of watching Anton bleed out by his side in the desert sand:

*I have these thoughts in my head like my life is over as I know it. It's actually a comforting one. Like after a disaster as big as this who I am as a person, how I interact with the world, will have to change. I pray that it's a trigger for me to become a better person. That I can give up the booze for one year & not sleep around anymore. These two I pray most often.*

Here, Jim sounds a bit like one of the desert fathers. Or poet Theodore Roethke, who penned this in one of his 277 spiral notebooks, "I'm tired of women. I want God."

## 15.

Days after Jim's execution, while sitting blankly in my sun-baked study, I cracked *The Unabridged Journals of Sylvia Plath*. I found this feral inscription scrawled inside—

*DJ*
*fuck it believe*
*Jimmy '06*

Mostly, I take this message as a sign to carry on with my writing. At others, I suppose it signals not to slam the door on God entirely. Jim never did. Deep in The *Unabridged Journals*, Plath muses, "Let me live, love, & say it well in good sentences."

## 16.

Jim's lowercased letter "a" almost always opens on top. According to graphologists, this signals a person who "is spontaneous, free, extroverted, honest . . . [One] unable to reserve confidences." In these inscriptions pre-dating his capture, Jim's handwriting strikes me as looser & wilder—un-prisoned.

When reading his Libyan prison journal, or referencing it, I often find myself referring to the "body" of the text. These five pages, then—standing 44" long, end-to-end, word count 5,578—stand in for Jim's body, given that his beheaded corpse was never recovered in Syria.

# 17.

A former rugby flanker, Jim was a guy's guy. A deep scar lined his right temple. He called people, "Bro," even some of his women friends. His attention often flickered, but you felt, when Friday night's roulette wheel landed on you, when you clinked bottles of Negra Modelo & pedaled together on bikes at night, when you slipped into a shadow fleet of hundreds on Pulaski Avenue to ride Chicago's inky streets—Kedzie, Humboldt, Western, Damen, Ashland, Milwaukee—you felt the bone-deep quality of Jim's love & brotherhood.

## 18.

Jim, now, is body-less, forever. Yet, every time I sit with these smuggled letters, his voice rises anew. It swells & falls. His watery script skitters.

These letters, they're the ticker tape of the missing. A ledger that forms & dissolves around me as I read it, a dead letter no longer dead.

Or one carried by passenger pigeon from a city on fire, written by a friend feared dead. Is that why I keep returning, over & again, like a pilgrim to the body of these pages?

*

...you've heard the executioners sing joyfully.
You should praise the mutilated world.

—Adam Zagajewski,
    translated by Clare Cavanagh

# Flight

*Prisoners in solitary confinement often talk of longing to see the moon—*

white-ringed & looming, it's a Beaver Moon, I see,
flooding the sloped lawn with smuggled light.

Jet streams arc. Laughter springs from the bonfire.
It feels luxurious, our drunkenness.

Is it a Beaver Moon for the smoky ring rippling out
like the circle made by a beaver smacking its tail

or is it a sign for hunters to whet the steel teeth of their traps?

Frost Moon & Mourner's Moon, it's also called.
Friends, we pass around objects & tell their stories—
    a Celtics hat,

a note from Iraq on the occasion of a wedding missed.

Had Jim escaped, once more, would he be sitting here
among us, lighting cigarettes off the fire, his face aglow?

Or, ever the stray, would he slip away, quietly rising

from the couch in dawn's dirty light, working the lock &
    door latch,

flagging down a dairy truck, jumping a westbound Greyhound,

crossing state lines, his most natural state to transmigrate—

to cross & cross, even in this one life, flaring from one phase,
one form, one body into the next.

## Video: Who Are the Libyan Rebels?

Desert wind buffets Jim's shotgun mic. Slack-shouldered, a
Libyan rebel stands in front of a truck draped with a red,
green, & black flag. "I leave my work ... um ... I am ... I work
accountant," the man says in a hushed, measured voice. Behind
wire-rim glasses, his coffee eyes look to the camera, then away.
"I have small company ... um ... I leave my work, my family to
came [sic] here with our brothers' forces ... to take our freedom."
A patchy beard spots his face. He wears a second-hand baseball
cap, not a military helmet. He wears a khaki dad coat, no flak
jacket. "We try to take our ... freedom," he says groping for the
words in English, clutching a rifle strap, slung over his shoulder,
with soft, bookish hands. "We are looking for ... a ... better
lives."[16]

---

16  Jim posted, "This also is Syria," pale, peach light washing the thou-
sand-year-old ruins of the Dead Cities at dusk. He flitted in & out of
Istanbul, crossing back into Syria, still staying for weeks, while many
reporters left after hours or days.

# This Also Is Syria

*—after a photograph of Aleppo's Salahaddin*
*neighborhood by Nicole Tung*

A mother looks out the window,
cellphone in hand,

as daylight honeycombs
the drapes.

Swifts flit past.
Wind chimes of beach glass.

*It won't be long.*

Strains of oud music rise
from a neighbor's radio.

Did the doorbell chime?
A woman across the way

rushes to the window.
Jets rip open the sky.

*It can't be long.*

Bottle-green glint of sea—
but how can that be?

Shouting in the street.
Flurry of footsteps

on stairs. Knocking.
Who is it?

*He can't be long.*

Inshallah.
What is it?

She opens the door.
A man steps into the frame:

*Zoha,* she says,
like a rush of birds.

He hands his mother
lamb wrapped in foil,

loose jasmine blooms.
As if her son's come back

from years at sea,
she cups his sun-kissed face,

as if he will never leave.
*It won't be long now,*

*it can't be long.*

## Visitation

We sit in a diner booth. Night
rain falls on the windows.
We talk of small things—
the ending of *Lincoln in the Bardo*,
our bus trip to Santiago de Cuba,
whether his VW Fox with flashing engine light
can make the rest of the trip.
We order breakfast.
Red-rimmed, his eyes scan the room.
When he gets up, I signal for the check
& glimpse, jagged & pink,
waxy scars daisy-chaining his neck.
I stare down the tiled hallway,
snap toothpicks, waiting for his return—
or will it be his fly-by-night escape?
The waitress tops off my cup.

# Daybook: April 17

A snake unhinges its jaws to gorge on an ostrich egg, even a small deer. Choking down something dirt-dry, almost larger than one's own body—that's what death feels like to the survivor, & death & death.[17]

---

17   Leaving Turkey at night in a car with darkened headlights to cross into Syria, Jim remarked to Nicole with a nervous laugh, "I was scared. There was a border guard calling us over & I thought *there goes our cameras.*" He escaped that time, but not the next.

## Journalist–Wayfarer–Lover of Books

I'm sorry to ask, again—
what do we do

with the body

& what do we do,
what do we do

without?[18]

---

18   After weeks & months, after 636 days since he was kidnapped, Jim
left his prison cell, blindfolded in a truck, his head shaved, for the sere
hills outside Aleppo & beyond.

# Vision in the Plate Glass of Mike's Gym

It's winter in Boston, diving-bell-dark by five,
& I'm running on a treadmill, earbuds in,
when I glimpse in the reflection next to mine,
an older man pumping his legs & arms
like a Nordic skier. It looks to be,
though I know it can't be, Bob. He's tall,
about my height. This man isn't tall.
I'd heard he was in bad shape. Is it him?
Wire-rim glasses, hair parted to the side.
It could be, but there's no way. He'd be bald,
or worse—hospice, sage burning bedside.
I watch him in the window. He steps carefully
off his machine, both Bob & Not Bob.
I cut my workout short, the belt slowing under me.
Astride the pec deck now, he finishes his reps.
Walking over, I half-salute, a grin spreading
on his face. *I couldn't tell if it was you,* I say.
*You heard?* he asks. I look at the freckled tops
of his legs. Then, again, at his plush head
of gray-brown hair. *My secretary said I looked jaundiced.*
*Fortunately, we caught it early.* He talks of chemo,
an operation to pluck the tumor from his gut.
A crescent of sweat rings the neck of his t-shirt.
*You look good,* I say. *You really do.*

When I look up, I see us repeated in the gym mirror,
me talking to Bob & Bob talking to me,
& I sense then, for an instant,
that there's a world beyond this one
& one beyond that, & on & on, each whirling
through a burning field of winter stars—
one with me & Bob in it, the others without.
Now, I'm talking fast, with a cascading urgency,
the kind you might use when talking
to a ghost in a dream. *I loved your collection*
*of stories. The world needs more of your writing.*
He laughs, talks of the get-well cards,
hundreds from patients & friends,
strung across his back porch. I can see them:
trembling prayer flags in a night wind.
I take his hand. He says he's writing.
I hold it in mine. It's large, bony, & warm.

## Shadow Act

*—for Ebele*

My head bowed
above the bone-white

bowl of the sink,
Ebele runs clippers

over my scalp
& neck before work,

teasing, *There's hardly
anything to cut,*

shearing small clumps
of hair like batting

from an old pillow
or the gray down

of a new goose.

\*

Married for years,
it's the first time she's cut my hair.

Luka & Olanna look on.
My wife's braids fall on my neck.

Every act has a shadow act.
*Run it up & down,* I offer.

*Don't make it streaky.*
Since the baby's still asleep,

she hurries in her work
& worries aloud the chattering

blades will nick my neck.

*

As Ebele's hand passes over me,
I think, again, of Jim—

before his beheading, his captors
shaved him like this—

then, I feel, once more,
my wife finger the spray

of freckles & liver spots,
softly chiding,

*Wear more sunscreen, love.*
Finished, she kisses my nape.

For every act, a shadow act.
The baby's now awake.

I offer to pay my wife
& she laughs a girlish laugh.

## Salt

I cradle our newest
in the waves.

*New, new,*
we call her,

she is that *new.*

New breast-
plate, new

sacrum, seven
islands of skull—

*

White sunhat,

tiny swimsuit—
palm trees stamped

blue on white,
like a Ming vase

I hug to my chest.

*

*Come in!*
I bark,

as brown surf
whipsaws

Olanna & Luka
across the beach,

who bob in
& out of sight.

Steel clouds bank—

a frothing swell
sloshes Nulia,

soaking her face.

*

I look to the beach.

Her mom's still asleep.
I wait for a shriek

but Nulia looses
a high magpie

laugh, licking &
licking salt

from her lips.[19]

---

\*

Death steals everything except our stories.

—Jim Harrison

# With all respects to heaven, I like it here

*—after a photograph of James Foley reading in a U.S. Army bunker,*
*Kunar Province, Afghanistan, 2010*


Back propped against a mammoth wall of sandbags,
you're reading *Let the Great World Spin*,
combat helmet cast off, aviator sunglasses set back on your head.

> *I sit here thinking about how much courage it takes to live an*
> *ordinary life.*

Legs crossed, you're wearing the pants your mom
bought you Christmas last. Your eyes gaze down at the page.
Lips slightly apart, a week's goatee sprouts.

> *There is, I think, a fear of love. There is a fear of love.*

Minus the shelling in the distance, the flak jacket yoked
around your neck, you could be reading in a cane chair
at a café anywhere—Phoenix, Pilsen, Istanbul, Mexico City.

> *The world spins. We stumble on.*

Serene as it seems, images flit & ghost across the page.
A gunner shot in the head on a high mountain pass
    floats above
Philippe Petit now reclining on the wire, now upright.

*I was trying, really trying, to pray, get rid of my lust, rediscover*
*that innocence. Circle of circles.*

You stole my books, Jim. I stole yours. Fifty-fifty you're reading
a copy you filched from me. We never said what we meant
outright.

*Read this*, we said, instead, *You gotta fuckin' read this.*

*

## Postscript: A Note about James Wright Foley (1973–2014)

During his lifetime, American journalist James Foley reported from conflict zones around the world, ranging from Iraq to Afghanistan. He dispatched stories and videos for a variety of news agencies including *Stars & Stripes*, *GlobalPost*, and *Agence France-Presse*. James's reporting stood out for its clear-eyed humanity, rugged lyricism, and boots-on-the-ground perspective.

In the field, James pushed to the frontlines to get his story, whether riding in a dump truck with Libyan rebels or embedding with U.S. Army National Guard troops on tour in Afghanistan. For his reporting, James received the "Best Online Coverage of Breaking News Award" from the Overseas Press Club in 2011.

During the Libyan uprising, Gaddafi's forces kidnapped James and his fellow reporters Manu Brabo and Clare Morgana Gillis in April 2011. South African photographer Anton Hammerl, who was traveling with the group, died from gunfire in the field. James and his fellow reporters spent 44 days imprisoned before being set free. James traveled home to the United States but returned to conflict reporting only months later. He set off, again, to Libya and then crossed into northern Syria to report on the raging civil war.

James disappeared outside of Aleppo, Syria, along with British reporter John Cantlie on Thanksgiving Day 2012. Different factions held James during his brutal captivity and moved him frequently. James' imprisonment dragged on for nearly two years, despite a rescue attempt launched by U.S. Special Forces. On

August 19, 2014, the extremist militant group ISIS beheaded James and videotaped his execution. The film was viewed by millions. To date, his body has not been recovered.

*

# Notes

Footnote 1 quotes Carl Sandburg's poem "Chicago."

"August 17" references David Finkel's book *Thank You for Your Service*, which follows U.S. soldiers after they return from service in Afghanistan. It's a companion volume to *The Good Soldiers*.

"glimmerings" comprises a lyric essay reflecting on the letters that James Foley penned as a prison journal while imprisoned by the Gaddafi regime for 44 days. The journal itself contains several cramped, hand-written pages on hotel stationary, which James smuggled out in his shoe, following his captivity by Gaddafi's forces. The essay quotes additional sources including: *Emily Dickinson: The Gorgeous Nothings*, edited by Jen Bervin and Marta Werner; James Foley's short story "Notes to a Fellow Educator"; Walt Whitman's *Memoranda During the War*; Hisham Matar's *The Return*; Daniel Rye Ottosen's *The ISIS Hostage*; *The Unabridged Journals of Sylvia Plath*, edited by Karen V. Kukil; and Theodore Roethke's *Straw for the Fire: From the Notebooks of Theodore Roethke*, edited by David Wagoner.

"Nothing Is More Beautiful than the Ruin of a Beautiful Thing" paraphrases what the French sculptor Auguste Rodin said about Michelangelo's raw and unfinished sculpture *Pietà*.

"Sparrows," originally composed during James Foley's 636-day imprisonment in Syria, now includes found poems from James

Foley's Libyan prison journal. In some instances, the language appears exactly as it does in James' journal. In other cases, I have reordered and rearranged it.

Section 16 of "Sparrows" includes a paraphrased line from a speech given by Berkeley student activist Mario Savio.

"Al-Fatiha" cited in "Sparrows" refers to the "The Opening" or "The Opener," which is the first prayer of the Koran. Its seven verses are a prayer for the guidance, lordship, and mercy of God. James Foley recited it with other prisoners while held captive in Libya.

Footnote 11 on page 63 quotes James Foley directly from a *Global-Post* video that he dispatched from Libya.

"Video: Who Are the Libyan Rebels?" draws on a video that Jim created for *GlobalPost.*

"This Also Is Syria" pulls its title from James Foley's Twitter post in which he shared out a picture of the Dead Cities at dusk. The poem is written in response to a picture taken by photojournalist Nicole Tung, which was featured on James Foley's website, "A World of Troubles."

*"With all respects to heaven, I like it here"* quotes passages from Colum McCann's novel *Let the Great World Spin.*

# Publication Credits

*Academy of American Poets:*  "In the Absence of Sparrows"

*Barrow Street:*  "catalogue of accidents," "Storm Damage," "Shadow Act," & "Salt"

*Forklift, Ohio:*  "For Olanna" & "Missing"

*Hanging Loose Press:*  "Foley Artist: Sound Effects for an Unmade Short Film"

*Hinchas de Poesia:*  "Knight of Swords," *"Protect Me from What I Want,"* & "Nothing Is More Beautiful than the Ruin of a Beautiful Thing"

*jubilat:*  "Wayfarer"

*The Southern Review:*  "Vision in the Plate Glass of Mike's Gym"

*Tin House:*  *"Inshallah"*

Following James Foley's execution, "In the Absence of Sparrows" was published and featured in a number of publications and media outlets including *PBS NewsHour*, *The Boston Globe*, *The Washington Post*, NPR, *Slate,* and elsewhere.

# With Thanks

Special thanks to the Foley family for their belief in this project and for allowing me to draw from Jim's Libyan prison letters. The world is a better, safer place thanks to the James Foley Foundation and their tireless advocacy to bring hostages home and their work to prepare conflict journalists to do their jobs as safely as possible.

Big love to the friends of James Foley: Rick Cohen, Don Cipriani, James Savage, Mike Joyce, Jon Racek, Brian Jordan, Heather MacDonald, Anuj Shah, Tom Durkin, Anders Hopperstead, Brian Oakes, Rich Griffin, and Mike Foley. Our boisterous annual gatherings have always picked me up, even in the most bruising of times. I look forward to toasting Jimmy, once more, on the banks of Lake Winnipesaukee and reading these poems together, fireside.

My literary agent Wendy Strothman and the team at the Strothman Agency have worked tirelessly to help find a home for these poems. They believed in this project, even when my own belief flickered. It's been a wonder to work alongside the attentive, thoughtful Jesse Nathan at McSweeney's. Big thanks to Amanda Uhle and the entire McSweeney's team for bringing this book to life. Thank you for helping me "say it well with good sentences."

Many of these poems were written at the Writers Room of Boston. Thank you, Debka, Geert, David, Mary, Mark, and others for your counsel and encouragement. Muchísimas gracias to other friends and colleagues who offered sound advice and under-the-hood tinkering: Scott Challener, Yago Said-Cura, Jeffrey Harrison, Dana Alsamsam, Charles Coe, Brian Jordan, James Savage, and Tom Durkin.

A big shout out to my peer-to-peer writing group: Cammy Thomas, Emily Wheeler, Vicki Murray, Christine Casson, and others who passed in and out over the years. I appreciate the warm embrace of the Boston branch of the Warren Wilson College MFA Program alumnae community. Brava to Debra Wise and the team at the Underground Railway Theater at Central Square, where Ebele and I got the chance to present a multi-media performance of this book as a work-in-progress. Thanks, too, to Erica Lee, Jon Demiglio, and Bob DaVies for their inspired collaboration over the years. Noel and Elle: I'm grateful for your friendship.

Additional thanks to the City of Boston for a Boston AIR Fellowship in 2018. Thank you, Joan Houlihan, Martha Rhodes, Ellen Doré Watson, and the attendees of the Colerain Manuscript conference. I'd like to extend my gratitude to the Fine Arts Work Center in Provincetown for their summer workshop offerings. This work was supported in part by finalist Artist Fellowship awards from the Massachusetts Cultural Council in 2018, 2020, and 2022.

Big props to GrubStreet and its community of writers, where I had the good fortune to teach while crafting these poems. I savored the chance to learn alongside my students. During this time, I've felt lucky to pass my days working alongside brilliant and inspiring teams at 826 Boston and Mass Poetry.

During the writing of this book over the course of a decade, three of my family members passed away including my father, Dr. Thomas Brock Johnson; my mother, Betsy Young Johnson; and my sister, Sarah Elizabeth Johnson. Their spirits walk and haunt these pages, too. Mom, Dad, and Sal: I like to think you'd be proud of this book. My brother Mark: I look forward to our next adventure together and appreciate your unflagging support.

To my wife Ebele, lovely and steadfast mate: thank you for taking me and Jimmy in on New Year's Eve in a New York City blizzard. To my kids, Olanna, Luka, and Nulia: when you're old enough to read this book, I hope, in small ways, that these stories and poems will bring back your Uncle Jimmy. Thank you, and love to all.

## The James W. Foley Legacy Foundation

Proceeds from the sale of this book will benefit the James W. Foley Legacy Foundation. The Foundation advocates for the freedom of all Americans held hostage abroad and promotes the safety of journalists worldwide. Learn more about this important work by visiting: jamesfoleyfoundation.org.